30 and not married!

Life hits hard on a single lady in her 30s

TONY ALBERT

COPYRIGHT

CONTENTS

CHAPTER 1

In friends circles, and with family and loved ones, special attention is always brought to the ones that are still single at 30, "why don't they bring anyone to Christmas, are they going to be alone forever, are they already a crazy cat lady" what have you! But you never hear anyone bring special attention to what it's like to be in a long-term relationship at 30 and not be married or have any kids. If anything at all, people just guilt trip you immediately, "when are you going to make us grandparents", or "I bet you're next", or other comments about how lucky we are because their marriage basically just sucks. (That definitely makes it all so much more enticing.)

30 used to be a significant age for young women, if not the milestone. Getting married in your 30s might simply be the

new standard, although turning 30 used to feel like a ghost in the distance, things seem to be changing. The typical marriage age has been in the 20s for many years, but things appear to be changing. As your twenties begin to fly by, you shouldn't worry if you're not even close to getting married.

Waiting longer to be married is getting more and more common, both statistically and socially. This tendency reflects both the best and a few of the slightly more challenging aspects of contemporary life. So how much has the marriage age changed historically? And why are more people waiting a little longer to be married? What you should know is as follows.

Statistics simply prove it.

People are actually marrying later than ever, even though it seems like everyone around you is starting to get married in their early 30s. The average age of marriage in the UK has now surpassed 30 years old. Many cite the average age of men and women who marry in the US as being 29 and 27, respectively, as evidence that the average marriage age has been rising. That is accurate based on the most recent data, but it does not reflect the current state of affairs. Given the trend toward older marriages, it is likely that our average marriage will enter the 30s in the near future if it hasn't done so already.

It's a Mirror of Our Times.

People are getting married later for a variety of reasons, and this reflects our period in both positive and negative ways. Women tend to marry younger than men, in part due to sexism and the promotion of spinsterhood, but also because historically speaking, women were less likely to receive as much formal education, let alone attend college or pursue a job. It is a testament to how much better things are for women now that some of them are delaying marriage. We may choose to put off getting married while we concentrate on other aspects of our lives because we have more freedom and options now.

It's Not a Lack of Romance Thing

We shouldn't start worrying about the hookup culture just because we're getting married later. People are still in committed relationships, and the number of cohabiting, non-married couples is growing. According to the Pew Research Center, 18 million Americans lived with their partner but were not married in 2016. To put it in perspective, since 2007, there has been a 29 percent increase. People are now demonstrating their dedication in other ways.

It Provides More Time for Reflection

One benefit of delaying marriage a little bit is that it may offer some individuals more time to come to terms with who they are and who they want to spend their lives with. It's wonderful if you knew what sort of person you wanted to be when you were 21 and found the ideal partner, but I know that I changed a lot in my 20s and wasn't ready to be in the kind of relationship I am in now until I was a little bit older. That extra time is essential for some folks.

From Person to Person, it Differs

The likelihood is high that when you read this, you're thinking, "Yeah right, all of my pals were married by 26." And that may be the case. Although these figures illustrate general tendencies, individual differences and even those between regions and religions still exist. While some religions can promote earlier marriage, people in urban regions typically marry later than those in rural ones. The point is that even though getting married in your 30s may soon become the new standard, you shouldn't feel uncomfortable or out of place if that doesn't at all reflect your life. You might wed when you're twenty, forty, fifty, or never.

CHAPTER 2

Being over 30 and unmarried isn't all that simple. While some people give in to pressure to get married young for various reasons, you walk around with a beacon of hope as you wait for "the moment" to dawn on you, with no regrets about the delay. The only issue is annoyance brought on by others who are eager to discredit you and take every chance they get to mock you(apparently, their way of showing concern). You are the lady who is the topic of conversations that begin, "She's well over 30 and single," and you are also the object of other people's envy. Consider this: You are single, unmarried, and happy.

It's not a yardstick for life; it's simply marriage. At a certain age, girls are expected to view marriage as their ultimate goal in life and it is treated as a standard. But it's acceptable to believe otherwise. Do it when the time is perfect and not when you witness others taking the jump or when someone suggests you do the same to avoid being referred to as the "wedding curse.

People frequently get married in order to complete something, not realizing that it is only the beginning of a relationship and not the end of something that needs to be completed. Marriage is a commitment combined with responsibility, not an obligation. Age is not a factor. What's up with the "oh, she's old enough" stone-age mentality?
There is no appropriate age for marriage; you can be mature in your 20s and can manage a relationship. Then again, you could be a 30-year-old who is utterly immature for relationship. Maturity and age are two separate things. Marriage should be decided upon by sensible factors, not by age!

How people develop emotionally, physically, and financially varies from person to person. It is more important to get married when you are ready, willing to accept the responsibility and commitment of marriage, and most importantly, when you find the right life partner. Marriage is not something that should be arranged at a "particular" age set by society.

Making sure matters. The secret to a happy existence is, indeed, that. We advise you to take some time for yourself and not walk down the aisle if you have no idea how far your emotions can go and more significantly, if you have no idea how to deal with the devil.

These are the "proper" reasons to get married if you are certain that you want companionship, a close sexual and emotional connection, the capacity to love and be loved, a fulfilling relationship over an extended period of time, etc. But you'd better think twice and choose not to be married if you want to get married because you're worried about growing old alone, you're lonely (which has nothing to do with being with someone!), you want financial stability, etc. "

In our society, marriage is the only accepted method for a man and woman to live together and formally be in a "relationship." It's about being happy. Most people look for the ideal man or lady. However, it is OK to live a happy single life until you discover the appropriate partner.

CHAPTER 3

The word "happy" is often associated with tension. But isn't contentment directly inverse to compromise and directly proportional to happiness?

How is it possible to relate "being single or being married" to the word "happy"? Yes, marriage is a ton of fun and happiness, but does that imply that only a married person is happy?
Happily single seems to be a coping method for someone who doesn't want to admit that he might dearly miss the company and a love partner. He, therefore, utilizes this as a defense or an explanation to feel better about himself. Happiness is a work in progress that can be attained with or without marriage.

What pressure, you ask? A million aunts will be using you as a "Miss Unmarried" case study while rolling their eyes in scorn. In actuality, having such conversations is simply antiquated and cultural.

Let folks know that before you say "I do," there are specific requirements that must be met. When you compare yourself to others, pressure is frequently self-created. If you are clear about what you want, you will be able to handle it. Because people make terrible decisions, a lot of marriages are in jeopardy. And why do they act in that way? because they are unsure of their values and identities. You can simply state, "I haven't found what I am looking for," if you are clear.
The pressures will continue. It's up to you how you respond to such pressures.

You can decide to succumb to the stress-inducing loop that results from not finding the right partner, or you can deal with societal and familial expectations by subtly letting them know that you won't become emotionally attached to someone who doesn't meet your needs. You have every right to live your life how you choose since it is your life.

Don't give up looking until you find a companion who meets all your needs. You can be forceful and let your family know what criteria you used while selecting a companion. Nothing matters as long as you are certain of who you want and how you want it. Additionally, avoid social (particularly family) circumstances where you can end up being the victim of endless whys, hows, and buts.

Giving in to the constant pressure, feeling overwhelmed, and being unable to function can either result in an emotional collapse, making you an even weaker person, or it will ultimately lead you to take the incorrect action by saying yes to the incorrect person.

It concerns Mr. Right-for-You. The typical bunch makes the huge error of waiting for Mr. "Oh-So-Right" and, while seeking the same, rejecting "Mr. Right for me."

CHAPTER 4

Although the final decision lies with you and no one else, you should keep in mind that delaying marriage has its drawbacks as well. We advise against overdoing the choosing process when you're on the right track and consider marriage to be a serious step to take.
You should keep in mind that your options won't expand as you age, so being logical and crucial while choosing.

Any marriage will also experience adjustments. That in no way implies that you marry someone you detest, aren't attracted to, or don't get along with. The fact that marriage is not everything must be kept in mind. If you discover the ideal partner who makes the path of togetherness more enjoyable, it truly maybe everything.

Like many women, I spent the majority of my twenties debating whether or not I even wanted a traditional marriage and family. I would have said, "Eww, why would I have kids when I could devote my life to more important things, like blogging and attending subpar sex parties?" if you had asked me about starting a family two years ago. I'm now, though, thinking, "I'm too lazy to go out. I might as well simply have a family.

It's obvious that some people desire to be single. Simply put, they are not now interested in entering into a committed relationship. Others are single as a result of their own circumstances. They can have recently ended a committed relationship or they might have dated constantly but failed to meet someone with whom they truly clicked. Here are several unconventional solutions to the perplexing "why am I still single?" especially those over 30, who are searching.

It's difficult to avoid feeling victimized when it comes to dating and relationships. After all, people can be harsh, and although it's not always your fault, you will nonetheless suffer harm. However, contrary to what we frequently believe, we actually have greater control over our romantic destiny. Although we rarely realize it, we greatly contribute to creating the world in which we live. In reality, we have a choice as to whether we want to view our lives as victims or decide to take control of them. Focusing on what we can influence rather than what we can't help us. We can become aware of the numerous ways we shape other people's responses to us, including unfavorable ones. What internal challenges do I need to overcome, then, for the single person yearning for love?

Most people have experienced interpersonal pain. We all run the risk of developing different levels of resentment and becoming defended with time and difficult experiences. This process starts in our early years, long before we start dating when harmful encounters and family dynamics cause us to build walls or view the world through a lens that may have a detrimental effect on us as adults. We may develop a greater sense of isolation and self-protection as a result of these adaptations. In our adult interactions, we might avoid showing too much vulnerability or dismissing people too quickly.

When we choose mates based on our defenses, we frequently make less-than-ideal relationship decisions. By choosing someone who isn't emotionally available, we run the risk of creating an unhappy relationship. We frequently hold our partner responsible for the breakdown of the relationship because this process is largely unconscious. Without realizing it, we frequently experience devastation or hurt after receiving numerous rejections.

We frequently feel pickier and more judgmental as a result of our defenses. This is especially true when we've experienced unpleasant experiences, such as being duped or rejected by someone we had a strong affection for. Many women begin to think things like, "There are no decent men out there" or "All the good ones are taken." Men could think things like, "You can't trust a woman," or "Women are just out to get you." When we first meet someone, we could have inflated expectations for a partner or be able to immediately see their shortcomings. We often dismiss a variety of potential mates before even giving them a chance when we are skeptical or distrusting of the world. Without ever considering how that person might make us happy in the long run, we consider dating a certain type of person to be "settling."

CHAPTER 5

People tend to burrow more and deeper into their comfort zones as they become older. The fact that modern women are becoming more accomplished, successful, and independent is a very beneficial trend. It is also simpler for both men and women to construct a bubble from which it is challenging to escape as they become more comfortable, whether financially or practically. It may feel more difficult to take chances or put oneself out there. Many of us may prefer to stay in our pajamas after a stressful day at work than venture out into the uncharted territory of meeting new people. Our critical inner voice frequently prompts us to stay inside or in a safe place. The self-calming advice from this inner coach is to "just stay in tonight and relax.

On your own, you'll be OK. Have a wine glass. Watch the program you enjoy.

The issue with this voice is that it will eventually start talking back to you, thinking things like, "What a loser you are, home alone again. For the rest of your life, you'll be alone. You are not growing older. You won't be liked by anyone. Many of the things we do to "comfort" ourselves end up making us feel horrible because they prevent us from pursuing the things in life that we genuinely want. It's crucial to avoid getting comfortable and to consistently combat the effect of our judgmental inner monologue. By making an effort to get out into a public, smile, make eye contact, and let friends know we are looking for someone, we should take action and let them know. To learn new things about ourselves and what makes us happy, we should try new things and even date different individuals.

As the years go by, we frequently create dating rules for ourselves. We essentially "write down" what we have learned, but what appears to be true on paper isn't always true in practice. When we follow guidelines based on our past, we run the risk of perpetuating a pattern of unsatisfying romantic partnerships. I know a woman who formerly dated a man with whom she had wonderful chemistry. She decided to give up hunting for a guy she had a deep connection to or attraction to after it didn't work out. She made "sensible" decisions instead, which led to her finding much less fulfilling relationships. When it comes to dating, it's critical to avoid establishing rigid standards or accepting others' norms.

One of the most crucial things we can do when looking for a loving companion is to remain open. Yes, we could get injured, but if we don't take chances, we have a lower chance of meeting someone with whom we could truly share a future. Game-playing and relationship rules frequently go hand in hand. They may cause us to act less sincerely and authentically and to isolate ourselves from our emotions. On the other side, maintaining an open and honest relationship will help us locate one that is far more genuine and lasting.

Although finding love is a difficult endeavor, it is always preferable to travel this path alone. Fighting the internal tendencies that prevent us from achieving our goals is crucial. We cannot protect ourselves from the outside world or prevent harm to ourselves. Everybody has weaknesses, and these weaknesses become more obvious when people become close to one another. Therefore, developing closeness is a courageous battle that is eventually worth fighting for in our relationships as well as within ourselves daily.

www.ingramcontent.com/pod-product-compliance
Lightning Source LLC
LaVergne TN
LVHW020546160826
845677LV00015B/4231

9798354053797